"I know not why or where North Dakotan jokes began," writes author Mike Dalton. "When I moved to Montana seven years ago everyone was telling them. As a morning radio announcer I use jokes as my forte. Listener contributions to my collection gave me over 1,200 'airable' North Dakotan jokes (and many more that are not compatible with juice and toast). This book is a distillation of the best (and maybe the worst) . . . "

THE NORTH DAKOTA JOKE BOOK

Mike Dalton

Drawings by MAL

A JOVE BOOK

This Jove book contains the complete
text of the original hardcover edition.

THE NORTH DAKOTA JOKE BOOK

A Jove Book / published by arrangement with
Lyle Stuart Inc.

PRINTING HISTORY
Lyle Stuart edition published 1982
Jove edition / October 1983

ISBN: 0-515-07357-1

Jove books are published by The Berkley Publishing Group,
200 Madison Avenue, New York, N.Y. 10016.
The words "A JOVE BOOK" and the "J" with sunburst
are trademarks belonging to Jove Publications, Inc.

PRINTED IN THE UNITED STATES OF AMERICA

DEDICATION
Special thanks to the State of North Dakota.
Without it this book wouldn't exist.

Foreword

Throughout my twenty years of traveling in the radio business I have found that there is a universal need to tell a joke at someone else's expense. In Wyoming they tell "Greenie" jokes about their neighbors in Colorado who have green license plates. In New York they tell "Iowa" jokes. In Canada they tell "Newfy" jokes about the residents of Newfoundland. For reasons I cannot understand they tell "Montana" jokes in Florida. Here in Montana we dwell on the exploits of our eastern neighbors in North Dakota.

For the most part the North Dakotan is of Norwegian/Swedish descent. Works very, very hard in a very hostile climate and has a very limited sense of humor. Knowing that North Dakotans cannot laugh at themselves makes the jokes about them even funnier.

I have had many people tell me they have bought my books to send to their in-laws in North Dakota. The gift has not been well received in most cases. And that in fact was why they were sent . . . they knew their in-laws could not take a joke.

I know not why or where North Dakotan jokes began. When I moved to Montana seven years ago everyone was telling them. As a morning radio announcer I use jokes as my forte. Listener contributions to my collection of jokes soon gave me a wealth of over 1,200 "airable" North Dakotan jokes (and many hundreds more that are not compatible with juice and toast).

The collaboration of Malcolm "Mal" Hancock on the art work has been a joy. Mal is an internationally known cartoonist from Great Falls. His work appears regularly in everything from *Boys' Life* to *Playboy*. His visual perception of the typical North Dakotan tells many stories.

Over the past six years 25,000 copies of my five North Dakota booklets have been sold, primarily in Montana. This book is a distillation of the best (or maybe the worst) of those booklets.

MIKE DALTON

THE NORTH DAKOTA JOKE BOOK

The North Dakotan came home early from work one day and found his wife with another man. The North Dakotan was infuriated. He got his pistol and put the barrel to his own head. His wife and the other man began laughing hysterically.

"Quit laughing!" he yelled. "You're next!"

What do North Dakotans have printed on the soles of their shoes?

This Side Down.

Did you hear about the North Dakotan who broke his arm raking leaves?

He fell out of the tree.

One day a North Dakotan in Montana was desperate to rent a house. He was so desperate that he decided to rent a Montanan's outhouse. The day after he moved in the Montanan noticed there were *two* TV antennas on the outhouse roof instead of one. He asked the North Dakotan why there were two. The North Dakotan told him, "Because I couldn't afford the rent by myself, so I sublet the basement."

If they cut 250 bras in half you have 500 beanies with chin straps. Leave the bras intact and you have 250 pairs of North Dakotan earmuffs.

Why do North Dakotans have such flat foreheads?
Every time they don't know the answer to a question they hit themselves on the forehead.

Why did the two North Dakotans get their luggage mixed up at the airport?
They both had brown paper bags.

There was the North Dakotan who bought *one* snow-boot for winter.

He heard there was going to be only one foot of snow.

A North Dakotan was building a garage and went to the lumber yard to buy some 2x4's. The lumber yard man asked the North Dakotan, "How long do you need your 2x4's?"

"I'm building a garage," said the North Dakotan, "so I'll need them for a long time."

What did the 1975 Miss North Dakota have that no other contestant had?

A wart on her nose.

What do you get when you cross a North Dakotan with a gorilla?

A retarded gorilla.

Dear Son,

Just a few lines to let you know that I am still alive. I am writing this letter slowly because I know that you cannot read fast. You won't know the house when you get home—we've moved.

About your father, he has a lovely job. He has 500 men under him. He is cutting grass at the cemetery.

There was a washing machine in the new house when we moved in, but it isn't working too good. Last week I put 14 shirts into it, pulled the chain and I haven't seen the shirts since.

Your sister had a baby this morning. I haven't found out whether it is a boy or a girl, so I don't know whether you are an Aunt or Uncle.

Your Uncle Dick drowned last week in a vat of whiskey in the Bismark Brewery. Some of his workmates dived in to save him, but he fought them off bravely. We cremated his body, and it took three days to put out the fire.

Your father didn't have much to drink at Christmas. I put a bottle of castor oil in his quart of beer. It kept him going until New Year's Day. I went to the doctor on Thursday and your father went with me. The doctor put a small tube in my mouth and told me not to open it for 10 minutes. Your father offered to buy it from him.

It only rained twice last week. First for 3 days, and then for 4 days. Monday it was so windy that one of our chickens laid the same egg four times.

We had a letter yesterday from the undertaker. He said if the last installment wasn't paid within 7 days, up he comes.

Your Loving Mother

P.S. I was going to send you $10.00 but
      I had already sealed the envelope.

What would you call six North Dakotans in a circle?
A dope ring.

Definition of a North Dakotan car pool:
Seven North Dakotans carrying a Volkswagen to work.

Why aren't there any garbage trucks in North Dakota?
They use them for campers.

Did you hear about the North Dakotan who was stabbed 20 times in the head?

He was trying to eat with a fork.

Two North Dakotans were passengers on a four-engine plane. Suddenly one engine quit and the pilot announced that the plane would now be fifteen minutes late. A short time later another engine quit. The pilot announced they would be thirty minutes late. Then the third engine quit and the pilot announced that they would be one hour late. At this point the one North Dakotan said to the other, "Boy, if the fourth engine quits we could be up here all day."

During the Sun River flood of 1975 a North Dakotan was observed standing on the 14th St. S.W. bridge in Great Falls with a toothbrush. He was asked what he was doing with the toothbrush in his hand.

The North Dakotan replied, "I'm waiting for the Crest."

A NORTH DAKOTAN
HITCHHIKING IN THE RAIN

Did you hear about the North Dakotan daredevil motor-cycle rider? He tried to jump the motorcycle river canyon on a snake.

The North Dakotan went into the tack shop to buy a saddle. He was asked if he wanted an English saddle without a horn or a western saddle with a horn. The North Dakotan replied, "I'll take the western saddle without the horn. I won't be riding in any heavy traffic."

Why can't North Dakotans raise chickens?
They plant them too deep.

Did you hear about the North Dakotan Evel Knievel?

He tried to jump fourteen motorcycles with a Mack truck.

Two North Dakotans were walking to Seattle from Minot on the railroad tracks. They got to Shelby and one North Dakotan said to the other, "Boy, I'll sure be glad when we get to the bottom of these stairs."

The other North Dakotan said, "Yah, me too. I'm tired of these low hand rails."

Definition of a North Dakotan bowling ball:
A three-holed brick.

What's the North Dakotans' answer to birth control?
They take the sacks off their wives heads.

Did you hear about Uncle Leon of Dickinson? He found a magic lamp and the genie inside gave Uncle Leon the Midas touch. Everything Uncle Leon touched turned into a muffler.

Did you hear about the North Dakotan who tried playing Russian Roulette with an automatic rifle?

A drunk North Dakotan leaves the neighborhood late one night and takes a shortcut through the graveyard. He stumbles into an open grave and passes out. A little while later another North Dakotan wanders by and hears moaning from down in the grave.

The North Dakotan in the grave moaned, "Oooohhh, I'm so cold."

The other North Dakotan looked down into the grave and said, "No wonder. You kicked all the dirt off."

There was an exciting football game between North and South Dakota. Halfway through the fourth quarter a train went by and tooted its whistle. The South Dakotans thought that was the end of the game and they left the field. Four plays later the North Dakotans scored.

What did the North Dakotan say when he found a pile of milk cartons out in the middle of the field?

"Hey, I found a cow's nest."

Why don't North Dakotans eat pickles?
They get their heads caught in the jar.

Two North Dakotans were walking down the road when a seagull flew over and dropped a "prize" on the head of one of them. The other North Dakotan quickly ran into the house and came running out with a roll of toilet paper. "Forget it," said the bomb victim. "That seagull is probably five miles away from here by now."

A North Dakota high school senior won first prize in the school's scholastic test. His mom asked him how he won.

"Easy. The question was, how many legs does a hippo have. I was the closest, I said three."

When visiting North Dakota, if a robber threatens to blow your brains out if you don't give him your money—don't give him the money. In North Dakota you can live without brains but you can't live without money.

WORD HUNT

**We've hidden four words in this word puzzle.
Can you find them?**

N. D. DEPARTMENT OF EDUCATION

D	U	C	K
D	U	C	K
D	U	C	K
D	U	C	K

What has an IQ of seven?
Eight North Dakotans.

Why are North Dakotan airline stewardesses always so tired?
From running alongside the plane holding up pictures of clouds.

After a long war with Montana, the North Dakotan army was weary and depleted of supplies. The General stood before his tired army. "I have some good news and some bad news," he said. "First the good news. Everybody gets a change of underwear." There was much cheering among the troops.

"Now the bad news," he continued. "Lieutenant Smith, you change with Sergeant Watson. Private Jones, you change with . . ."

North Dakotans think Taco Bell is a Mexican phone company.

Next time you're in North Dakota visit the North Dakotan Hilton. They have a revolving restaurant in the basement.

A North Dakotan went to the doctor and complained of being listless. The doctor told him to run ten miles a day and call him in eight days. Eight days later the North Dakotan called the doctor and said, "Doctor, I sure feel a lot better, but I have a problem."

The doctor said, "You ran ten miles for eight days didn't you?"

"Yes," said the North Dakotan. "Now I'm eighty miles away from home and I don't know how to get back."

Why doesn't North Dakota have any pharmacists?

They can't find a typewriter that will type on those round bottles.

What's long, green and tastes like a carrot?
A North Dakotan pickle.

There was a North Dakotan who got water skis. He gave them away because he couldn't find a lake with a hill in it.

How do North Dakotans lose five pounds in five minutes?
They take a shower.

How are North Dakotan ears like steam shovels?
They pick up a lot of dirt.

What's the capital of North Dakota?
About $3.85.

Why did Canada get all of the Frenchmen and the U.S. get all the North Dakotans?
Canada had first choice.

What's the difference between a North Dakotan grandmother and an elephant?
About seven pounds.

What is the most dangerous, highest paid job in North Dakota?
Riding shotgun on a garbage truck.

A North Dakotan went ice fishing for the first time. He brought home a 200-pound block of ice. His wife tried to fry it and they both drowned.

The symphony orchestra from Minneapolis went to Bismarck for a concert. Two North Dakotans in the back of the auditorium were seeing who could recognize the most instruments. They named them all except the slide trombone. The one North Dakotan said to the other, "There must be some trick to it. He ain't really swallowing it."

What did the North Dakotan housewife say when the garbageman said, "Any garbage today?"

She said, "Yes, I'll take three bags."

Did you hear about the North Dakotan atheist? He quit because there weren't any holidays.

There was a sheriff in Williston who got a wanted poster from Helena showing a wanted bank robber in six different pictures. The sheriff wired the Helena police a week later saying, "I have five of the suspects in custody; should apprehend the other before the week is over."

There was a North Dakotan who thought he would be a good actor because his leg had been in a cast once.

There was an airplane with a Frenchman, a Montanan and a North Dakotan on board. The pilot told the three passengers that one of them would have to bail out or they would crash. The pilot told them to do it for the love of their country. The Frenchman volunteered and, as he jumped from the plane, he yelled "Vive la France!"

A while later the plane was still in trouble and again the pilot begged one of his passengers to jump out for the good of his country. So the Montanan pushed the North Dakotan out.

What is the best thing to come out of North Dakota? Highway Two.

There are two North Dakotans standing on top of a ten-story building. One is wearing a white shirt and one a red shirt. If they jumped off at the same time which one will hit the ground first?
Who cares?

Why don't they allow North Dakotans to join the Army?

They don't make square helmets.

Two North Dakotans were walking down the street when they met a Catholic priest with his arm in a cast. The priest told them he had broken his arm when he slipped in the bathtub. After the priest left, one North Dakotan asked the other, "What's a bathtub?"

"How should I know," replied the other. "I'm not a Catholic."

There was a North Dakotan father who told his sons he wanted to be buried at sea. When he died, his sons took the body from Minot to the Atlantic Ocean. All three sons drowned while trying to dig a grave.

What happens to North Dakotan snow tires in the summer?

They melt.

How does a North Dakotan count his cattle?

He counts their feet and divides by four.

Have you heard about the North Dakotan scientist who has invented a device that will allow you to see through a wall three feet thick?

He's going to call it a "window."

The library on the campus of the University of North Dakota burned yesterday. It burned both books. The fire was especially tragic because one of the books hadn't been colored in yet.

While engaged in a political conversation a North Dakotan was asked what he thought of Red China. The North Dakotan replied, "It doesn't look too bad with a purple table cloth."

It takes three North Dakotans to play hide-and-go-seek.
One goes and hides and the other two try and figure out who left.

The next time you're in North Dakota notice that most North Dakotans have clear plastic garbage cans. Why? So when they're in the mood they can go window shopping.

Why do seagulls have wings?
So they can beat the North Dakotans to the garbage dump.

Did you hear about the North Dakotan who smiled every time there was lightning? He thought he was having his picture taken.

The coach at the University of North Dakota was upset because his star quarterback had flunked a math test. He asked the math professor why he had flunked. The math professor told the coach that the quarterback had written on his test that $5 \times 7 = 33$. The coach got very mad at the professor and said, "Oh, come on professor. Give him a break. He only missed the right answer by one."

Two North Dakotans were driving down a country road when they spotted another North Dakotan out in the middle of a wheat field in a rowboat. One North Dakotan laughed and said, "Shouldn't we go get him?" The other one said, "No. How can we? We don't have a rowboat."

Two North Dakotans were fishing on one side of the river and were catching nothing. Two Montanans were fishing on the other side of the river and catching a bunch. One North Dakotan said to the other, "They may be catching more fish, but they're cheating. They cut a hole in the ice."

What do you get when you cross a North Dakotan with a mermaid?

A 150-pound carp.

There was a North Dakotan who lived right on the Montana border. One day some surveyors came to his door to inform him they had made a mistake years before and now the North Dakotan actually lived in Montana. "Oh good," said the North Dakotan. "I don't think I could stand another one of those North Dakota winters."

Three North Dakotan hunters were out one day hunting. They tried to identify a pair of tracks they found. The first North Dakotan argued that they were bear tracks. The second North Dakotan was sure they were rabbit tracks. Before they could make up their minds what the tracks were a train ran over them.

Did you hear about the North Dakotan loan shark? He loaned out all of his money and skipped town.

How does a North Dakotan spell "Farm"?
E-I-E-I-O.

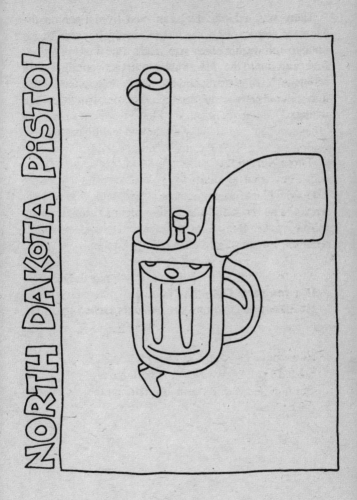

There was a couple buying a house from a contractor. They walked through the house telling the contractor which color to paint each room. Each time they told him a color he would stick his head out the door and yell "Green side up!" After a while the couple asked if that was some type of code for the colors they wanted.

"No," said the contractor. "I have two North Dakotan college students outside laying the sod and I have to keep reminding them that the green side goes up."

There was the farmer outside of Bismarck who plowed his fields with a steamroller. He wanted to grow mashed potatoes.

What's the difference between a rich North Dakotan and a poor North Dakotan?

A rich North Dakotan has two cars jacked up in his front yard.

How do you keep a North Dakotan busy?

Put him in a round room and tell him there's a penny in the corner.

Why do they keep a garbage can at North Dakotan weddings?
To keep the flies off the bride.

Why do North Dakotans have such pretty noses?
Because they're hand-picked.

Who invented the limbo?
A North Dakotan trying to sneak under a pay toilet door.

What do you call a North Dakotan who marries a pig?
A social climber.

Did you hear about the North Dakotan who looked in a lumber yard for the Draft Board?

Sign on the back of a North Dakotan garbage truck: "We cater wedding parties."

Did you hear about the North Dakotan who wore a union suit because his wife was having labor pains?

A Montanan asked the North Dakotan how he liked watching his first football game.

The North Dakotan replied, "It was OK but I can't understand why they went to so much trouble and pain for 25¢."

"What do you mean?" asked the Montanan.

The North Dakotan then said, "Well, through the whole game everybody kept yelling, 'Get the quarter back, get the quarter back.'"

Why don't they give North Dakotans more than a ten-minute coffee break?

It's too hard to retrain them.

A North Dakotan crossed the border once a week into Montana and bought bales of hay for $1.00 each. He took them back to North Dakota and sold them for $1.00 each. He soon found that he was losing money rapidly on his business venture. But, being a smart North Dakotan, he came up with a way to quit losing money. He bought a bigger pickup truck.

The North Dakotan said to his neighbor, "You should pull your shades at night. Last night I saw you kissing your wife through the living room window."

"Ha, ha," said the North Dakotan. "The joke's on you. I wasn't even home last night."

Why did the North Dakotan housewife sit and cry in her kitchen? Her husband went out to shoot crap and she didn't know how to cook it.

A Montanan was driving down the road when he saw a North Dakotan standing outside his burning house. The Montanan asked the North Dakotan why he wasn't trying to put the fire out. The North Dakotan said, "I'm not worried. I'll build a new house out of all the lumber I have stored in the attic."

Did you hear about the Montanan who had a large brain tumor that had to be removed? When the doctors removed the tumor they accidentally removed the brain too. Three days later the Montanan escaped from the hospital. Two years later guess where they found him —teaching school in North Dakota!

Did you hear about the North Dakotan who wanted to go to the rock concert? The ticket prices were $5.00 in advance and $6.00 at the door. He decided not to go because he didn't want to pay $11.00.

The wheelbarrow was invented to teach North Dakotans how to walk on their hind legs.

Who won the North Dakotan beauty pageant? Nobody.

Why do all North Dakotans have a mark in the middle of their forehead?

Because everybody's been touching them with ten-foot poles.

If there was a race between the Easter Bunny, Santa Claus, a smart North Dakotan and a dumb North Dakotan, which one would win?

The dumb North Dakotan. There's no such thing as the Easter Bunny, Santa Claus or a smart North Dakotan.

Did you hear about the North Dakotan who thought Manual Labor was the President of Mexico?

Why are there so few North Dakotan suicides?

It's not easy to get killed jumping out of a basement window.

What is the smallest book in the world?

The North Dakotan Book of Knowledge.

Did you hear about the North Dakotan who thought Sherlock Holmes was a housing development?

Did you hear about the North Dakotan who thought Ernest Tubbs was a place to take a bath?

What is big, sluggish, stupid and has a trunk?
A North Dakotan on vacation.

A group of North Dakotans were going hunting. They agreed that if they became lost they were to fire three shots into the air, wait fifteen minutes, then fire three more shots, and so on. One of the North Dakotans did become lost. Two days later they found him and asked why he hadn't used the instructions and fired three shots. "Well, I did," said the North Dakotan, "but I ran out of arrows."

Definition of a North Dakotan intellectual: One who reads to himself without moving his lips.

What is the perfect gift for the North Dakotan who has everything?
A garbage truck to put it in.

A North Dakotan scientist has discovered a new substance that removes foreign particles from the skin. He's going to call it "soap."

Did you hear about the North Dakotan terrorist who tried to blow up the school bus?
He burned his lips on the tailpipe.

Did you hear about the North Dakotan who studied four days for his urine test?

Who discovered North Dakota?
The Roto Rooter man from Sidney, Montana.

A North Dakotan went to the store and bought a chain saw. Three days later he returned to the store with the saw and complained that the saw wasn't working right. In three days he had only been able to cut down two trees. The first time the store clerk pulled the starter rope the saw motor started. The North Dakotan asked, "What's that noise?"

Did you hear about the North Dakotan who went on an elephant hunt but was forced to turn back because he got a hernia from carrying the decoys?

If a North Dakotan throws a pin at you what should you do?
Run! Chances are the hand grenade in his mouth will explode any second.

How do you sink a North Dakotan battleship?
Put it in the water.

Did you hear about the North Dakotan Model 460 air conditioner?

Drive sixty miles an hour with all four windows down.

The phone rang one day and the North Dakotan answered it and then hung up. His wife asked him who it was. The North Dakotan said, "It was the operator. She said it was long distance from New York. I told her 'it sure is' and hung up."

Why does it take three North Dakotans to pop corn?

It takes one to hold the pan and the other two to shake the stove.

How did the North Dakotan pilot figure out that he had landed with his wheels up?

He had to taxi to the terminal at full throttle.

Did you hear about the North Dakotan Evel Knievel who tried to jump over thirteen roto tillers with his high-powered tractor?

He might have made it except for one thing. He forgot to unhook the plow.

An employee of North Dakotan Bell was trying to measure the telephone pole but couldn't figure out how to climb up the pole. Someone suggested that he lay the pole down on the ground and measure it. The North Dakotan phoneman didn't like that idea. He said, "We want to measure how high it is, not how long."

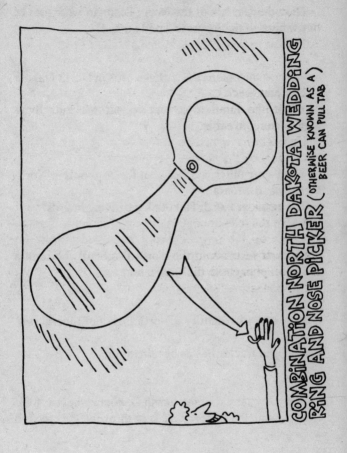

COMBINATION NORTH DAKOTA WEDDING RING AND NOSE PICKER (OTHERWISE KNOWN AS A) BEER CAN PULL TAB

Did you hear about the North Dakotan who tried to throw himself on the ground and missed?

Why do they paint the garbage cans in North Dakota orange and black?
When the families go out to eat the kids think they're going to eat at the A & W.

What's the difference between the cesspools in North Dakota and Montana?
The pools in North Dakota have diving boards.

Did you hear about the North Dakotan who took a roll of toilet paper to the crap game?

How can you identify a North Dakotan funeral procession?
The lead tractor has its headlights on.

Did you hear about the North Dakotan who was fired from the banana factory? He kept throwing the crooked ones away.

What is the North Dakotan state bird?
The Fruit Fly.

Did you hear about the North Dakotan who always backed off the bus?
He heard someone was going to grab his seat.

Did you hear about the North Dakotan who was so lazy he married a pregnant woman?

There was a North Dakotan scientist who was experimenting with the hearing of frogs. He cut off one leg and told the frog to jump. It did. He cut off a second leg and told him to jump again. He did. The scientist cut off the third leg and told the frog to jump again. He did. The scientist then cut off the fourth leg and again commanded the frog to jump. This time the frog did not jump. The North Dakotan scientist concluded that when you cut off all four legs on a frog he loses his hearing.

A North Dakotan took his dog hunting for the first time. Instead of jumping into the water to retrieve the birds, the dog walked on the surface. The North Dakotan got rid of the dog because he couldn't swim.

The mailman said to the North Dakotan, "Is this your package? The name is obliterated."
The North Dakotan replied, "No. It can't be mine. My name is Murray."

What do you call it when you shoot a flaming arrow into a garbage can?
A North Dakotan shishkabob.

Why don't North Dakotans ever go ice fishing?
By the time they get done cutting a hole in the ice big enough for their boat, they're too tired to fish.

In 1887 there was a fierce battle between the armies of Montana and North Dakota. The North Dakotans kept throwing sticks of dynamite at the Montanans. The Montanans lit them and threw them back.

Why does every North Dakotan shoe have "TGIF" stamped on it?

It's a reminder that "Toes Go In First."

Who do North Dakotans think John Boy is?

Someone who cleans bathrooms.

A North Dakotan was killed by a weasel. He was walking down the railroad tracks and didn't hear the weasel.

What does it say on the bottom of a North Dakotan pop bottle?

"This side down."

The North Dakotan said to the Montanan:

"If you can tell me how many chickens I have in this sack, I'll give you both of them."

The North Dakotan bride wore something old, something new, something borrowed, something blue, something orange, something lilac, something chartreuse, something red, something . . .

A new zoo has been proposed that will be the largest in the world. They're going to build a fence around North Dakota.

Did you hear about the North Dakotan race car driver who came in last at Indianapolis last year? He averaged 4.5 miles per hour. He had to make seventy-five pit stops . . . three for fuel, two to change tires and seventy to ask directions.

Why can't you get ice cubes in North Dakota?
The old lady who had the recipe died.

On the first day of football practice the head coach walked up to the North Dakotan, handed him a football and asked, "Can you pass this?" The North Dakotan football player examined the ball carefully and said, "Gee coach, I don't even know if I can swallow it."

Why did the North Dakotan drive around the block twenty-four times?

His blinker was stuck.

If a North Dakotan and a Montanan jump off an eight-story building at the same time, which one will land first?

The Montanan. Because the North Dakotan got lost.

Definition of "North Dakotan matched luggage": Two shopping bags from the same store.

The Governor of North Dakota signed three bills into law last week. He would have signed more but his crayon broke.

A North Dakotan went on vacation to Hawaii. When he got off the plane a hostess put a Hawaiian lei around his neck and said, "Aloha from Hawaii."

The North Dakotan responded, "Murphy from Minot."

What is red, green, purple, blue, yellow and orange? A dressed-up North Dakotan.

How did the first 1,000 North Dakotans get into Montana from North Dakota?

The first North Dakotan swam across the Yellowstone River.

The other 999 walked across on the dead fish.

What is the North Dakotan state flower?
The Tumbleweed.

Did you hear about the North Dakotan who thought "no kidding" was birth control?

A North Dakotan heard that most accidents occur within ten miles of home, so he moved.

What did the North Dakotan do for fun on Saturday night?
He called up the weather bureau and asked in a whispering voice, "Is the coast clear?"

Why did they cancel the North Dakotan birthday party?
Someone flushed the punch bowl.

Did you hear about the North Dakotan who put iodine on his paycheck because he got a pay cut?

Why did the North Dakotan buy the new car?
He couldn't keep up the payments on the old one.

Why don't they have North Dakotan elevator operators?
It's too hard to teach them the route.

What is a North Dakotan cookout?
A fire in a garbage can.

Definition of gross ignorance: 144 North Dakotans.

Why did the North Dakotan sleep on his stomach?
He heard the Japanese were looking for a new naval base.

About eighty-five years ago a Montanan and a North Dakotan got caught stealing horses. Because there were no trees around to hang the horse thieves from, the sheriff tried to hang them from a bridge.

The Montanan's rope broke, and he swam to shore and escaped.

As they were placing the rope around the North Dakotan's neck, he said to the sheriff, "I hope this is a strong rope. I can't swim."

Preparation H: North Dakotan lipstick.

A young North Dakotan became quite worried about his baldness. A friend recommended that he get a transplant. A month later he showed up with a heart on his head.

In the other 49 states electric watches sell well. But not in North Dakota. They can't find anyone who makes extension cords long enough.

Headline in the *Fargo Tribune* last week: 2 North Dakotans Drown While Trying to Put a Basement in Their Ice House.

Two North Dakotans decided to become truck drivers and they went to take the truck drivers test. One question asked what they would do if they were going down a long, steep hill and the brakes failed. One North Dakotan wrote, "I'd wake my partner up. He's never seen a bad wreck before."

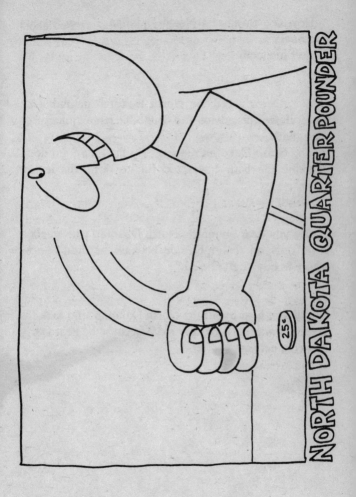

How do you cure a North Dakotan of chewing his fingernails?

Pull his teeth.

The doctor asked the North Dakotan patient if he had followed his advice and drunk the lemon juice after a hot bath.

The North Dakotan replied, "By the time I got done drinking the bath I was too full to drink the lemon juice."

Did you hear about the North Dakotan who smelled good only on the right side because he didn't know where to buy "Left Guard."

Did you hear about the North Dakotan who took his pregnant wife to a grocery store because he heard they had free delivery?

Just the other day two seagulls were observed flying over North Dakota upside-down. Upside-down because they couldn't find anything worth pooping on.

If there were two Santa Clauses on the roof, how could you tell which one is the North Dakotan?
He's the one with the Easter basket.

How can you tell if a North Dakotan is level headed?
When the snoose runs out of both corners of his mouth.

What is the North Dakotan state tree?
The Telephone Pole.

There were two North Dakotans talking and one said to the other, "Do you know what Easter is all about?"

The second one said, "Oh, that's when that little fat man dresses in red and brings all the toys."

"No, no," said the first one.

"Oh," said the second one. "It must be when you go out and shoot a turkey and have a big dinner."

"No, no," said the first. "It's when they put Jesus on the cross and then put him in a cave and rolled a rock in front of the door. Then three days later, the rock rolled away and Jesus stepped out and saw his shadow and there was six more weeks of winter!!"

Did you hear about the North Dakotan who got stranded on the escalator during a power outage?

A North Dakotan had two horses but couldn't tell them apart. First he cut the tail off one of the horses but it grew back. He tied a bell on the neck of one of the horses to tell them apart but the bell fell off. At last the North Dakotan decided to measure the horses to see if maybe one was taller than the other. Sure enough. The white horse was five inches taller than the black horse.

A North Dakotan and a Montanan agreed to meet in Calgary to go hunting. Two weeks after the Montanan arrived in Calgary the North Dakotan showed up. The Montanan asked the North Dakotan what took him so long. The North Dakotan said, "Everytime I stopped at a gas station there was a sign that said 'clean restrooms.' So I did."

Did you hear about the North Dakotan hijacker who hijacked a submarine, demanded $500,000 and a parachute?

You know you're in North Dakota when Colonel Sanders has a Norwegian accent.

Two North Dakotans were out fishing in a boat and enjoying good success. As they prepared to return to shore they agreed that one of them should mark the spot so they could return to the same location the next day. The spot was marked and they set out for shore. When they arrived one North Dakotan asked the other, "How did you mark the spot?"

"I put an X on the boat."

The other one replied, "That was dumb. What happens if we don't get the same boat?"

A cowboy from Wyoming went into the men's shop and bought seven pairs of underwear. The clerk wanted to know why he bought seven. The man replied he wanted one pair for each day of the week. Later that day a Montanan entered the same store and bought eight pairs explaining he wanted one for each day of the week plus one pair to wear on washday. The same day a North Dakotan entered the same store and bought twelve pairs of underwear. The clerk asked him why he bought twelve pairs. "Because," said the North Dakotan, "I want to have one pair for each month of the year."

Did you hear about the North Dakotan who wanted to become a stud?

He wrapped himself around a snow tire.

A North Dakotan went into a pizza parlor and ordered a 12-inch pizza. The waitress asked him if he wanted it cut into eight or twelve pieces.

"Eight pieces," said the North Dakotan. "I'm not hungry enough to eat twelve."

Two Montanans and a North Dakotan had a bet as to who could stay in a pigsty with the pigs the longest. The first Montanan lasted two days and left. Three days later the second Montanan left. Two days after that the pigs left.

The next time you see a North Dakotan with blisters on his face you'll know what he was doing. He was bobbing for French fries.

"Do you file your fingernails?"

"No," said the North Dakotan, "I throw them away."

In North Dakota they think Shirley Temple is a synagogue.

The North Dakotan from the country drove into Fargo for the first time and stopped at the traffic light which was red. When the light turned and the "walk" sign lit up the North Dakotan got out of his car.

Adam was a North Dakotan. He had to have been. Only a North Dakotan could eat an apple with a naked girl sitting next to him.

The highway patrolman pulled the North Dakotan driver over and told him he was driving on the wrong side of the road. The North Dakotan had the right answer: "I know I was driving on the wrong side. The other side was full."

They gave the North Dakotan girl three guesses and she still couldn't tell which way the elevator was going.

Do you know why the North Dakotan spent two weeks in the revolving door?
He couldn't find the doorknob.

What do you call 500 North Dakotans at the beach?
The Bay of Pigs.

North Dakotans think Gatorade is welfare for crocodiles.

The North Dakotan was asked what he thought of the Indianapolis 500. The North Dakotan answered, "They're all innocent."

Did you hear about the North Dakotan who stepped in cow manure and thought he was melting?

What is the difference between a North Dakotan's cowboy boots and a Montanan's cowboy boots?

Montanan cowboy boots have cow "stuff" on the outside.

An unemployed North Dakotan got a job working for the Montana Highway Department painting the yellow stripe on the highway. The first day he painted a mile. The second day half a mile. The third day a quarter of a mile and the fourth day fifty yards. His boss asked the North Dakotan, "How come each day you painted less and less?"

"Well," said the North Dakotan, "each day I got farther and farther away from the bucket."

The other day a North Dakotan drove his new semi-truck off a cliff. He told the police he wanted to check his air brakes.

The University of North Dakota just had astro turf put on the football field. Their reason was a little unusual. They put down astro turf to keep the homecoming queen from grazing.

The University of North Dakota had astro turf installed on their football field and it cost $250,000 more than the astro turf at Montana State University.
Reason: The North Dakotans had a sprinkling system installed.

When the surgeon general's report came out saying that cigarettes caused cancer in mice, the North Dakotan put his cigarettes up on a high shelf where the mice couldn't reach them.

A North Dakotan won a gold medal in the 76 Winter Olympics in Austria. He was so proud of it that he took it to a shop in Innsbruck and had it bronzed.

There was a North Dakotan minister who was very intelligent. In fact, he had so many degrees that his North Dakotan parishioners called him "Father Fahrenheit."

Did you know it takes 2001 North Dakotans to sail a boat? One to steer and 2000 to pull the lake.

Of course North Dakota has an official state flower. Mildew.

If you see two planes flying in a snow storm how can you determine which one is the North Dakotan? The North Dakotan plane will be the one with the chains on the propellor.

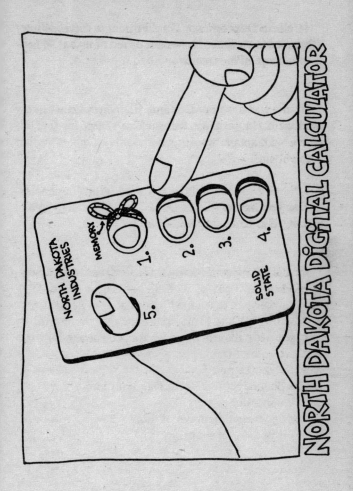

NORTH DAKOTA DIGITAL CALCULATOR

Here's some progress. They no longer have square wheels in North Dakota. Now they're triangular. They got rid of one of the bumps.

Ad in a Billings paper: Wanted: a North Dakotan to stand on the top of a semi-truck to watch for underpasses. Need six per week.

A North Dakotan mother got tired of putting nametags on her son's shirts so she had his name legally changed to "machine washable."

North Dakota is not known for its excess of grazing land for cattle. To cope with the shortage a North Dakotan farmer has developed a special cow he calls his "60-40 cow." It has to go sixty miles per hour with a forty-foot-wide mouth in order to get enough to eat.

How do you get ten North Dakotans into a VW?
Throw in a dime.
How do you get them out of the VW?
Throw in a bar of soap.

All North Dakotan fire trucks have a Dalmatian that rides to all fires. That's the only way the North Dakotans can find the fire hydrants.

They use birth control pills in North Dakota. They feed them to the stork.

A man walked into a North Dakotan store and asked for sealing wax. The North Dakotan clerk replied, "This must be a joke. You don't really want to wax the ceiling do you?"

A North Dakotan dog wandered into the woods the other day and all the trees wet on him.

There are CB radio operators in North Dakota too. Do you know how they say "10-4"?
"5-5-2-2."

One day a North Dakotan was asked if he wanted to be a Jehovah's Witness. "I can't," said the North Dakotan. "I didn't even see the accident."

The North Dakotan meteorologists get confused easily. Every time it gets cloudy they can't figure out how the rain gets through the clouds.

Did you hear about the North Dakotan who planted his hands? He wanted to grow a palm tree.

One poor North Dakotan bought a bottle of Mennen After Shave lotion and the very next day was found dead in his bathroom. The autopsy revealed that he had slapped himself to death.

Here is how you make North Dakotan chocolate chip cookies.

It takes two people. One stirs the batter while the other squeezes the rabbit.

Even in a crowded room it's easy to identify a North Dakotan. He will be the one with the wrong end of the cigar in his mouth.

Did you ever stop to think why it is that North Dakotans have bananas and the Arabs have oil?

North Dakota had first choice.

Last week Bismarck police arrested a North Dakotan with several sticks of dynamite in his shirt pockets. The North Dakotan told the police, "I'm tired of Jake slapping me in the chest and breaking my cigarettes. When he hits me today he's going to get his hand blown off."

The North Dakotan obviously didn't understand when the lady in the bar told him she was a lesbian. The North Dakotan's response was, "Oh, how are things in Beirut?"

Then there's the story about the North Dakotan who had to buy a new garbage disposal.
The first one was full.

Two North Dakotans bought a brand-new Ford station wagon with wood paneling. When they got it home they removed the paneling. After observing their handiwork one North Dakotan said, "I think I liked it better in the box."

Montanans are forever taking advantage of North Dakotans. One Montanan sold a $2 parking ticket to a North Dakotan for $100.

How does a North Dakotan put on a stamp?
He licks the envelope.

How many in a North Dakotan funeral procession?
Seven. Six to carry the casket and one to drag the
body.

How did the North Dakotan hope to get steel wool?
By feeding his sheep ironized yeast.

A North Dakotan sat in a car wash one day for three
hours because he thought it was raining too hard to
drive.

After shovelling snow for several hours one North Dakotan said to his partner, "There must be an easier way to do this. I know. Let's burn it."

"No," said the second North Dakotan. "What would we do with the ashes?"

The North Dakotan went to the airport and asked for a roundtrip ticket. The ticket agent asked, "Where to?"

The North Dakotan thought for a second and then said, "Well, back here of course."

Did you hear about the North Dakotan burglar who broke two windows in the house? One to get in and one to get out.

A quick check of any North Dakotan phone book will reveal that Otto is by far the most common first name. Reason: There's only two letters for them to remember.

A panhandler approached a North Dakotan and asked, "Would you give me 50¢ for a sandwich?"

"I don't know," said the North Dakotan. "Let me see the sandwich."

A North Dakotan has developed a new parachute. It opens on impact.

A North Dakotan football player went to the chiropractor and demanded a 50% discount because he was a halfback.

What do you find in a North Dakotan's nose?
Fingerprints.

North Dakotan definition of "innuendo": An Italian suppository.

On the job application there was a blank to be filled in with the date of birth and the year. The North Dakotan filled in the blank, "Date: August 16. Year: every year."

I met a North Dakotan the other day who told me he'd give his right arm to be ambidextrous.

Then there was the North Dakotan football player who heard he was going to be a first round draft choice. He fled to Canada.

The North Dakotan skier swore he'd never ski again after his first attempt. He got his fanny frostbitten because he couldn't figure out how to get his pants on over his skis.

There will be a special TV show soon in North Dakota. It will be two hours long and feature a North Dakotan trying to count to 100.

The teacher asked the North Dakotan to count to five. The North Dakotan proceeded to count to five on his fingers. When asked if he could count any higher the North Dakotan raised his hand over his head and counted to five again.

Why do North Dakotan men have their elbows pierced?

So they can wear cuff links in the summer!

Why do North Dakotans eat beans every Friday night?

So they can have a bubble bath on Saturday.

Did you hear about the North Dakotan who thought a rebuttal was a fanny transplant?

The North Dakotan was asked in the restaurant if he preferred red or white wine. "It doesn't matter to me," said the North Dakotan, "I'm color blind."

Why do they bury North Dakotans with their rear ends sticking out of the ground?

So they can be used for bicycle racks.

One day a North Dakotan went into a chicken coop and lost his gum. He thought he found it three times.

One very contemporary North Dakotan carpeted his bathroom one day. He liked it so well that he got some more carpet and ran it all the way to his house.

Two North Dakotan state legislators were talking one day. "What do you think we should do about the prostitution bill before the Senate."

"I think if we owe it we should pay it."

"Did you see the eclipse last night?" asked the teacher.

"No," said the North Dakotan student. "It was so dark I couldn't see anything."

Question on history test: Where was Joan of Arc burned? North Dakotan's answer: "All over her body."

Then there's the story of the North Dakotan bank robber who strode into the bank, slammed down a $20 bill and demanded, "Give me all your brown paper bags!"

The North Dakotan farmer was lifting his hogs, one by one, up into his apple trees to graze on the apples. His neighbor came along and asked, "Doesn't that take a lot of time?"

The North Dakotan thought for a second. "No. What's time to a hog?"

**A
North Dakotan
Tying His Shoe**

Two North Dakotans were up on a barn roof one day fixing the roof. Their ladder fell down and the only way they could get down was to jump into a manure pile. The first North Dakotan jumped and his partner up on the roof asked how deep it was.

"It's up to my neck."

The second North Dakotan jumps and finds the manure is only up to his ankles.

"I thought you said it was up to my neck?"

The first North Dakotan said, "Well, it is if you jump headfirst like I did."

North Dakotan grandmothers take birth control pills. Do you know why?

They don't want any more grandkids.

The other day a North Dakotan jumped off the Empire State building in New York.

He apparently wanted to show his girl friend that he had a lot of guts.

Do you know what a mop is in North Dakota?

It's the state flag.

Once there were two North Dakotan farmers who used four donkeys to plow their fields. Three of the donkeys died. The North Dakotans heard that there were a lot of donkeys for sale in Texas, so off they went. The first Texan they talked to saw a good deal before him even though he was a watermelon grower and didn't have any donkeys.

The Texan said, "I don't have any donkeys, but I have some donkey eggs."

The North Dakotans bought four eggs (watermelons) and headed off for their ranch in North Dakota. Along the way the "eggs" fell out of their truck. By the time the North Dakotans got their truck turned around and returned to the broken "eggs" some jack rabbits were already eating the "eggs."

The North Dakotans thought the rabbits were baby donkeys. As they approached the rabbits took off running so fast that the North Dakotans couldn't get near enough to catch them. After they caught their breath one North Dakotan said to the other, "It's probably just as well we didn't catch those donkeys. I didn't want to plow that fast anyway."

The North Dakotans figured out what to do with their old fire truck when they bought a new one. They used the old one for false alarms.

Do you know what April 1st is?
North Dakota Day.

North Dakotan union members have it all figured out. They go on strike during their lunch hour so they won't lose any money.

Definition of a "goof ball."
A goof ball is a North Dakotan dance.

In the last couple of years abortions have become very popular in North Dakota. In fact, they are so much in demand there's now a twelve-month waiting list.

When the North Dakotan walked into the movie theatre the usher asked him if he wanted to sit downstairs or in the balcony. The North Dakotan said, "I don't know. What's playing in the balcony?"

Did you hear what the North Dakotan said when he saw the nude woman swim up to the river bank and get out?

"Boy, wouldn't she look good in a bathing suit?"

Last winter a North Dakotan tried to keep warm by building a fire in his kayak. The kayak burned. Moral of the story: You can't have your kayak and heat it too.

An unfortunate North Dakotan walked into the emergency room of the Fargo hospital with both of his ears badly burnt. The North Dakotan explained, "The phone rang and I picked up the iron by mistake."

The nurse asked, "How did you burn the other ear?"

"I did that," said the North Dakotan, "when I went to call the ambulance."

Seismologists now know why there are earthquakes in California. Every time a North Dakotan is buried the earth rejects the body.

What is an ice cube in a shoe box?
A North Dakotan refrigerator.

Here is a sure way to make a lot of money.
Buy all the Cheerios in Montana.
Take them to North Dakota and sell them as donut seeds.

The North Dakotan cut the hole in his carpet so he could see the floor show.

There was a North Dakotan from Grand Forks who didn't go to the christening of his nephew because he didn't want to see a baby get hit over the head with a bottle of champagne.

There is a real shortage of basketballs in North Dakota because no matter how much air they put in them they never weigh thirteen pounds.

Did you hear about the North Dakotan parrot who ate beans? He wanted to be a Thunderbird.

The North Dakotan motorist was explaining to the police officer how he had an accident with a tree.
"It wasn't my fault, officer. I honked my horn."

The North Dakotan locked his car keys in his car. He called the locksmith and said, "My keys are locked in my car. You've got to come over right away because it's starting to rain and the top's down."

It takes fifty North Dakotans to take a bath. Forty-nine spit in the tub and one washes.

How do you get a North Dakotan out of a bathtub? Simple. You turn on the water.

The North Dakotan went into town one Saturday and met a beautiful girl. They danced together all night. When the dance was over the North Dakotan asked the girl for her phone number so he could call her for a date.

"Capitol 3-1999," she said.

The North Dakotan thought for a moment and asked, "How do you make a capital 3?"

The Army has come up with a new mine detector. It's a North Dakotan. He sticks his fingers in his ears and starts walking.

The North Dakotan was with a group singing Christmas carols. "Leon, Leon," he sang.

The guy next to him nudged him and whispered, "Stupid, turn your book over—it's Noel, Noel."

What do you call good looking North Dakotan girls?
Lucky.

The weather in North Dakota:
Six months of cold and six months of lousy sledding.

A North Dakotan walked into a saloon and saw a moose head on the wall. He asked the bartender if it would be all right to go into the next room to see the rest of it.

For nearly three years two North Dakotans saved their money to go on a trip to Chicago. As they were travelling through Illinois they saw a highway sign that said "Chicago Left." The North Dakotans turned around and went home.

What did the North Dakotan airplane pilot do when he saw he was going to crash into the mountain?

He dumped his fuel tanks so he wouldn't have enough gas to get there.

In Minot the other day a North Dakotan died after refusing artificial respiration. He said he wanted the real thing.

The North Dakotan was asked how long it would take him to wash three basement windows.

He thought it would take at least eight hours. "It will take seven hours just to dig the hole to put the ladder in."

It was in North Dakota that the first hernia was successfully transplanted.

"Dear Grandma," wrote the North Dakotan. "Thank you for the rowing machine. I may have to return it though. It doesn't fit in the bathtub."

Turtleneck sweaters are very popular in North Dakota.

That's the easy way for North Dakotans to hide their flea collars.

We expect this hot item to
really catch fire with the public.

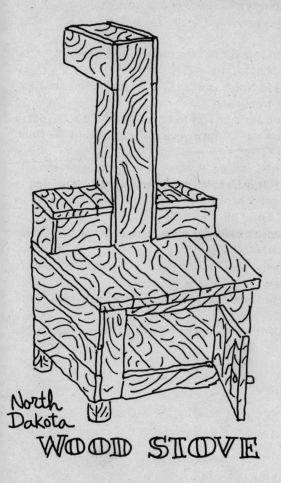

North Dakota
WOOD STOVE

Guaranteed to burn 5 hours.

On the job application form was a blank labelled "church preference." The North Dakotan wrote in the blank "red brick."

Sign in window of camera store in Bismarck:
"Flashbulbs for rent."

There's one sure way to keep a North Dakotan out of your back yard. Move your garbage cans to the front.

The North Dakotan told the librarian he wanted to read a good book. "Do you want something light or heavy?" asked the librarian.

"It doesn't matter. I have my car outside," said the North Dakotan.

Do you know how you can tell when you're in North Dakota?

You will see toilet paper hanging on all the clothes lines.

Why did the North Dakotan put holes in the top of his umbrella?

He wanted to see when it stopped raining.

A North Dakotan from Minnewaukan went to Minneapolis to see his first major league baseball game. As the North Dakotan was enjoying his first hot dog and beer, he heard someone behind him yell, "Hey, Ernie!" The North Dakotan stood up, turned around and looked. When he recognized no one he sat down and resumed eating. About two innings later, again the North Dakotan heard, "Hey, Ernie!" Again the North Dakotan stood up, turned around and looked. Again nothing. The third time it happened the North Dakotan stood up, looked around and then hollered back, "My name ain't Ernie!"

What's dumb, ugly and rings your doorbell all the time?

A North Dakotan Avon lady.

On a hot August day a North Dakotan was seen wearing two coats. When asked why he said, "The directions on the can said to put on two coats."

Did you hear about the North Dakotan whose father told him about the birds and the bees? The next day the North Dakotan was stung by a bee and he thought he was pregnant.

Why did the North Dakotan dig three holes to bury his dog?

The first two weren't deep enough.

What happened when the North Dakotan went out to water his calves?

His pants froze.

And then there was the North Dakotan who wanted to put an index in the front of the dictionary.

During the last Montana/North Dakota war do you know how the Montanans took over North Dakota?
The Montanan Army marched across the North Dakota border backwards and the North Dakotans thought they were leaving.

What is the most difficult decision a North Dakotan has to make when going to a formal party?
Whether to wear his red or green socks.

Did you know a North Dakotan needs two hands to eat a bowl of soup? He needs one to hold under the fork to catch the drippings.

There is a logical reason why the North Dakotan housewife fed her husband beans and pineapple:
She liked Hawaiian music.

North Dakotans think a Saturday Night Special is a bath.

A North Dakotan scientist has found a solution to the water shortage.
He gathered up all available water and diluted it.

North Dakotan bank robbers are easy to identify. They always wear a paper bag over their heads and ask the teller to put the money in a nylon stocking.

The North Dakotan knew his job was in jeopardy when they moved him to a smaller office that stopped at each floor.

ELEVATOR

North Dakotans don't eat M & M's. They get tired of trying to peel them.

Warning: In North Dakota if you don't pay your garbage bill they'll quit delivery.

Did you hear about the hip North Dakotan who put his radio in the oven?
He wanted to hear some hot music.

Definition of a galloping gourmet:
A North Dakotan running after a garbage truck.

A researcher at North Dakota State College has developed an artificial appendix.

Police Captain: "He got away, did he? Didn't I tell you to cover all exits?"
North Dakotan Cop: "Yes, sir. I did, too. But I think he must have walked out through one of the entrances."

A North Dakotan was invited to his wealthy girl-friend's home for dinner. When he walked into the house, the butler said: "Cocktails are being served in the library."

So he ran all the way downtown.

First North Dakotan: "Have you seen *Dr. Zhivago?*"
Second North Dakotan: "No, I go to Dr. Reynolds."

An absentminded North Dakotan farmer looked down and noticed that he was holding a rope in his hands. "I wonder . . ." he thought. "Have I found a piece of rope or lost my horse?"

With North Dakotan Airlines you can fly in one of three classes:

In first class they show a movie and give you a steak dinner.

In coach they show slides and give you a chicken dinner.

In the "no frills" section they pass around a picture of a peanut butter sandwich.

The North Dakotan's shirt was soaking wet when he picked up his date.

"Why is your shirt wet?" she asked.

The North Dakotan replied, "Well, the label inside says, 'wash and wear.'"

What do you call a North Dakotan born with half a brain?

Lucky.

Prairie Dog: Any girl from North Dakota.

A man went to a North Dakotan psychiatrist. "Doc, I think I'm schizophrenic."

"That makes four of us," replied the North Dakotan psychiatrist.

The waiter in a North Dakotan restaurant asked, "Is your steak tough, sir?"

"I don't know," said the customer. "I'm still cutting through the gravy."

At the Bismarck Chamber of Commerce meeting the treasurer reported a deficit of $100. One of the North Dakotan Chamber members stood up and said, "I vote we donate half of it to the Red Cross and the other $75 to the Salvation Army."

There was an ingenious North Dakotan who moved his house back fifty feet to take up the slack in the clothes line.

Two North Dakotans from Fargo went fishing in Canada. They caught one fish. When they got home, one of the North Dakotans said, "The way I figure our expenses, that fish cost us $400."

"Well," said the other North Dakotan, "at that price, it's a good thing we didn't catch any more."

How do you identify the bride at a North Dakota wedding?
She's the one with the braided armpits.

Scientists at the university of North Dakota are still looking for a cure for wheat germ.

There was a North Dakotan who thought a bar stool was something Davy Crockett stepped in.

There was a North Dakotan who wanted to see flying saucers, so he went to the truck stop and goosed the waitress.

Disgusted with his players during practice, the North Dakotan coach called them together and laid down the law. "Look men, I'm convinced that before we can make any further progress, we must go back to the fundamentals."

He reached over and picked up a ball.

"Now this," he said, "is a football. It . . ."

At this point a North Dakotan lineman interrupted: "Please, Coach, not so fast!"

In Las Vegas, a North Dakotan was running up and down putting dimes in parking meters. A curious bystander asked, "What are you doing?"

The North Dakotan replied, "I love this outdoor gambling."

There was a North Dakotan sitting out in the rain, holding out a tin cup. When asked why he was doing this, he said, "I heard the weather man say there was going to be a little change in the weather."

The North Dakotan didn't get to work until 11 o'clock one morning and his boss shouted, "You should have been here two hours ago."

The North Dakotan said, "Why, what happened?"

A North Dakotan pilot was enroute from Bismarck to Billings with 127 passengers. Bad weather forced them to circle Billings. As the fog continued, they kept circling for almost an hour. Finally the pilot announced over the P.A. system. "I have some bad news and some good news. The bad news is that we are running out of gas. The good news is, I'm parachuting down to get help."

The North Dakotan rushed home one night and happily announced to his wife: "Dear, now we don't have to move to a more expensive apartment. The landlord has raised our rent."

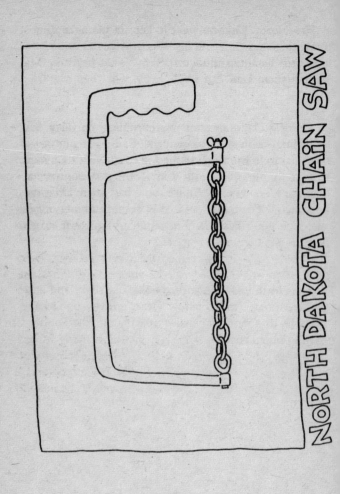

NORTH DAKOTA CHAIN SAW

Professor: "Do you want to help in the fight against malaria?"

North Dakotan Student: "Why, what have the Malarians done now?"

Three North Dakotans were arguing one day over how much dynamite to use to kill a pig. The number of sticks varied from one to twelve. The North Dakotan wanting six sticks finally won. The six sticks were attached to the pig, the fuse lit, and the North Dakotans ran and hid behind a rock. After the tremendous explosion the North Dakotans looked out from behind the rock and could see no trace of the pig.

"I told you so," screamed the North Dakotan who wanted to kill the pig with 12 sticks. "We didn't use enough dynamite and he got away!"

A North Dakotan was seen one night lying in bed and hitting his pillow with his fist. When asked why he was doing this he explained, "I can't fall asleep and I heard Dad say that he falls asleep as soon as he hits the pillow."

The North Dakotan space program is in trouble. Their astronauts keep falling off the kite.

A North Dakotan went to the doctor. After a lengthy examination the doctor said, "Take these pills two days running, then skip a day. Follow this routine for two weeks, then report back to me."

At the end of one week, the North Dakotan went back to the doctor. "I'm tired, doc," he complained. "That skipping wore me out."

A North Dakotan went to the new car dealer in Fargo and bought a fancy new $10,000 van. On his first trip out of town on the freeway he had a horrible wreck and totaled the van. When he regained consciousness, the North Dakotan told the highway patrolman, "Well, I was driving along and got hungry. So I put it on 'cruise control' and went to the back of the van to fix a sandwich."

What do North Dakotans do with their armies?
They put them in their sleevies.

Ad in the Grand Forks newspaper.
Wanted: Burned out light bulbs. I'm a photographer and I need them for my dark room.

Did you hear about the North Dakotan who was so far behind in his alimony that his ex-wife threatened to repossess him?

Before his first plane ride, the North Dakotan was told that chewing gum would keep his ears from popping during the flight. After finally landing he turned to his companion and said, "The chewing gum works fine, but how do I get it out of my ears?"

Have you heard about the ingenious North Dakotan who made counterfeit $2 bills?
He rubbed the zeros off the $20's!

If you want to make a lot of quick money sell snow to North Dakota. They use it for landfill.

A North Dakotan was drinking a glass of chocolate milk when he suddenly got a sharp pain in his eye.
Do you know what he did to get rid of the pain?
He took the spoon out of the glass.

General Custer stopped in Bismarck on his way out west to meet the Indians at the Little Big Horn. He told the Bismarck Chamber of Commerce, "Don't do anything until I get back."

They haven't.

You will probably never see electric cars in North Dakota.

The governor won't let anybody drive one because he's afraid somebody might trip on all the cords.

Did you hear about the North Dakotan who worked himself into a position of personnel manager of the company and interviewed his first job applicant.

"What was your major in college," he asked.

"Mathematics," the applicant answered.

"Well, say something in mathematics," the North Dakotan demanded.

"Pi R square," he replied.

"Wrong," said the Aggie. "Pie are round, cornbread are square."

What's yellow, stupid and wasteful?

A busload of North Dakotans going over a cliff with two empty seats.

Did you hear about the North Dakotan who was having trouble sleeping? His doctor prescribed some sleeping pills that he guaranteed would make the North Dakotan "sleep like a baby."

And they did. The North Dakotan woke up in the morning and found he had wet the bed.

Two hundred years ago today Uncle Fred Foonman of Fargo invented the toilet seat. Ten years later Uncle Fred made another invention—he cut a hole in the toilet seat.

Where is the safest place to hide money from a North Dakotan?
Under a bar of soap.

What do you get when you cross a North Dakotan with a watch?
A cuckoo clock.

North Dakotan matched crystal: Three empty peanut butter jars with the same label.

We celebrate March 17 in commemoration of St. Patrick's great and noble deed in driving the Norwegians out of Ireland. It seems that centuries ago, many Norwegians came to Ireland to escape the bitterness of Norwegian winters. Ireland was having a famine at the time and food was quite scarce. The Norse were eating almost all the fish caught in the area, leaving the Irish with nothing but potatoes.

St. Patrick, taking matters into his own hands like most Irishmen do, decided the Norwegians had to go. Secretly he organized members of the Irathicans (Irish) Republican Army to rid Ireland of Norsemen.

The Irathicans sabotaged all power plants in the hope fish in Norwegian refrigerators would spoil, forcing the invaders to a colder climate where the fish would keep.

The fish spoiled, as expected, but the Norwegians, as everyone knows, to this day thrive on spoiled fish.

Faced with failure, the Irishmen sneaked into the Norse fish storage in the dead of night and sprinkled the rotten fish with lye, hoping to poison the intruders. But, as everyone knows, this is how lutefisk was introduced to the Norwegians and they thrived on this lye-soaked smelly fish.

Matters became even worse for the Irish when the Norse started taking over the potato crop and making lefse. Poor St. Patrick was at his wit's end, and finally on March 17 he blew his cork and told all the Norwegians to go to hell. It worked. All the Norse left Ireland and went to North Dakota.

A young North Dakotan went to the Everglades of Florida on a sightseeing boat. While floating along he accidentally dropped his expensive camera in the water. As he reached down in the water an alligator reached up out of the depths and snapped off his arm at the shoulder. Later, in the hospital, as he recuperated from the amputation the North Dakotan called his father to tell him of the mishap. The North Dakotan's father was griefstricken when told about the loss of an arm. "Which one was it?" the father inquired.

"I don't know, Dad," replied the North Dakotan son, "if you've seen one alligator you've seen them all."

Did you hear about the North Dakotan who was half Japanese and half Norwegian?

Every December 7th he'd attack Pearl Olson.

"Father," said the North Dakotan student, "I flunked the geography test today because I couldn't remember where the Azores are."

The North Dakotan father replied, "Son, next time remember where you put things."

WARNING: When calling a North Dakotan on the phone, always whistle loudly in the phone and yell "OTHER END," so the North Dakotan knows which end of the phone to talk into.

What do they call a good looking girl in North Dakota?

Tourist.

There were two parachutists, one from Montana and one from North Dakota. They were making their first jumps. The North Dakotan jumped first, counted to ten, pulled the ripcord and his chute opened. The Montanan then jumped, counted to ten, pulled the ripcord . . . nothing happened. All of the time he is dropping quickly. The Montanan then pulled the emergency cord . . . nothing. He kept dropping. Before long he passed the North Dakotan. The North Dakotan looked down at the falling Montanan and immediately the North Dakotan began unbuckling his chute and hollered, "So you want to race, do ya?"

North Dakotan color TV: A keyhole into the next apartment.

Last winter there was a North Dakotan who was wearing a muffler to stay warm. That worked all right until someone started the car.

Why did the North Dakotan have his teeth pulled? So he'd have more gum to chew.

1st Man: Do you know how to talk North Dakotan?
2nd Man: Nope. Couldn't get the hang of it.
1st Man: How does it feel to be dumber than a North Dakotan?

How many North Dakotans does it take to eat a rabbit?

Three.

One to eat and two to watch for cars.

Two North Dakotan brothers strolled into a bar one night and were asked by the bartender, "Do you know what has four arms, four legs and two heads and is really stupid?"

The North Dakotans shook their heads.

"It's you and your brother," said the bartender, pointing at the two North Dakotans.

The brothers then decided to pull the joke on someone else, so they went to another bar where they met two brothers.

"Do you know what has four arms, four legs, two heads and is really stupid?"

The one North Dakotan replied, "Me and my brother."

The fire department in Bismarck got so many obscene phone calls that they got an unlisted number.

A new North Dakotan game:
Two North Dakotans go into a dark closet.
One sneaks out.
The other one tries to guess who's missing.

The North Dakotan Television Network is offering a new show next year about a big dog and his friend, a potato. The name of the new North Dakotan show is "Husky and Starch."

There was a North Dakotan water polo team at one time, but it was disbanded when one of their horses drowned.

Did you hear about the North Dakotan who fired his maid for being dishonest?

Two of the towels he swiped from the Holiday Inn were missing.

What magazine is banned in North Dakota?
Good Housekeeping.

Did you hear about the North Dakotan inventor who stayed up nights trying to find a cure for insomnia?

Then there's the story of the North Dakotan business-man who flew to New York and caught a cab to take him to Manhattan. As they were driving along the cab driver decided to see if it was true what he had heard about the intelligence of North Dakotans. The cab driver said to the North Dakotan, "My parents had three kids, one was my brother, one was my sister. Guess who the third one was." The North Dakotan thought, then said, "I don't have any idea."

"You dummy," said the cab driver, "it was me."

Upon returning home, the North Dakotan told his wife of the trip and said, "My parents had three kids, one was my brother, one was my sister. Guess who the third one was." The North Dakotan's wife didn't know.

The North Dakotan said, "The third one was some cab driver in New York."

A new restaurant has just opened in Minot. It's called the "Flaming Pit."

If you can't pay your bill they set your underarms on fire.

One North Dakotan was complaining to another.

"My wife tried a mudpack on her face. Looked great for three days. Then the mud fell off."

An enterprising North Dakotan got a job selling outhouses to farmers. He sold the one-holers for $150 and two-holers for $200 and, during the course of the summer, sold several hundred, because he guaranteed that they wouldn't stink. Before school started again in the fall, he decided to call on all his customers to be sure they were satisfied with the product. But, upon calling on the first farmer, he was astounded to see him boiling mad. "Say, young man," the farmer said. "Didn't you guarantee my outhouse wouldn't smell?" The North Dakotan agreed he had done so.

But, before refunding the farmer his money, the North Dakotan said he wanted to take a look to see if he could find the trouble. A few minutes later, the North Dakotan returned.

"No wonder," he exclaimed. "Look what you've gone and done in there!"

Everybody thinks Minot, North Dakota, is the end of the world.

Not really. But you can see it from there.

There is only one thing wrong with North Dakotan coffee. One month later you're sleepy again.

Two North Dakotans were sitting in a tavern drinking beer. One of them remarked, "Do you think Ali McGraw is her real name?"

The other North Dakotan, mulling over the question, sipped his beer a few times and matter-of-factly replied, "Do I think whose real name is Ali McGraw?"

North Dakotans think that a 280 Z is Dolly Parton's bra size.

Did you hear about the North Dakotan who argues that he should be allowed to march in the St. Patrick's Day Parade because he has green teeth?

What does every North Dakotan woman have that Raquel Welch doesn't?

A wart on her chin.

A North Dakotan is fishing on one side of the river, a Montanan is fishing on the other side. The Montanan asks the North Dakotan how to cross the river. The Montanan follows the North Dakotan's instructions and goes into the river over his head.

"Funny," says the North Dakotan, "I saw three ducks cross right there a little while ago."

Why does the new North Dakotan Navy have glass-bottom boats?

So they can see the old North Dakotan Navy.

Do you know where they print the North Dakotan obituaries in the newspaper?

Under "Civic Improvements."

North Dakotan newlyweds drove from Williston to Billings on their wedding night and went to their motel room. The North Dakotan groom kissed his bride and then started to go to sleep. The North Dakotan bride wakes him up, "This is our wedding night. I thought we'd go farther than this." So, the North Dakotan got up, packed the car and they drove on to Great Falls.

The opening game of the football season, the third-string guard on the North Dakota State football team asked the coach to wet down the field.

When asked why, the third-string North Dakotan replied, " 'Cause I want to go in as a sub, coach."

Did you hear about the intelligent North Dakotan? It was just a rumor.

A North Dakotan was to make arrangements for the burial of his brother. He had no luck in finding a suit for his deceased brother, so he rented a tux. For the rest of his life he kept getting a $30 monthly bill.

In North Dakota birthday cakes have no writing on them. They can't get the cake in the typewriter.

The mafia is training North Dakotans to be hit men. Two victims have already been found in North Dakota. They had their heads tied together and they had been shot in the hands.

A Montanan was selected by the North Dakotan Space Administration to go to the moon.

"How long will I stay?" asked the Montanan.

The North Dakotan replied, "Until we raise enough money to bring you back."

Did you hear about the North Dakotan who stopped soaking his dentures when he got his head stuck in the glass?

Two North Dakotans were sent up in a space capsule. During the flight around the earth one of them went on a scheduled space walk. During the walk, the door accidentally closed. The North Dakotan astronaut inside the capsule suddenly heard a rapping on the door. "Yah, who is it?" he inquired.

Did you hear about the North Dakotan who could count to ten? Would you believe five?

Did you hear about the North Dakotan who thought Noel Coward was a man who was afraid of Christmas?

North Dakotans think it's unlucky to be superstitious.

What do they call a thirty-five-year-old North Dakotan in the third grade? A genius.

A North Dakotan and a Montanan went into a bar for a drink. The Montanan ordered J & B on the rocks. The North Dakotan ordered a "13." "What's that?" asked the bartender. The North Dakotan said, "That's a Seagram's 7 and 7-Up, you dummy."

There was a North Dakotan who went to Minneapolis and read the big city newspaper for the first time. As he read the obituary page, he scratched his head and muttered, "That's mighty strange. The folks here die alphabetically."

A North Dakotan, when asked why he dragged a chain all over town, answered, "Have you ever tried to push one?"

This sign appeared on the wall of the North Dakota State University Library: "Due to the reorganization, the basement will be on the second floor. Half of the second floor will be on the first floor, but half will remain on the second. First floor will move to the basement. We suggest you ask for help." *True*.

Did you hear about the North Dakotan who thought High Cholesterol was a religious holiday?

There is no longer a driver education class at Bismarck High. The mule died.

Two North Dakotans were preparing for a math exam. One asked the other, "How many degrees are there in a circle?"

Answered the second North Dakotan after considerable thought, "How big is the circle?"

NORTH DAKOTA GARBAGE DISPOSAL

A North Dakotan walked into a drugstore in Grand Forks and asked the druggist for acetylsalicylic acid. The druggist says, "Don't you mean aspirin?"

The North Dakotan says, "Yeah, I can never remember that name."

You know you're in North Dakota when the state seal is a hockey puck.

What do 1776 and 1492 have in common?

They're adjoining rooms at the North Dakota Hilton.

A Montanan blacksmith hires a North Dakotan to help him. The blacksmith hands the North Dakotan a hammer and says, "Follow me around and every time I nod my head, you hit it." They buried the blacksmith yesterday.

You will never find a can of extra dry deodorant in North Dakota. The North Dakotans are afraid they'll get cracked armpits.

At a North Dakotan State football game last year a North Dakotan cheerleader got sick. A rather nervous substitute from a small Minnesota college was quickly drafted. Determined to do well, he looked up at the stands packed with cheering North Dakotans, cleared his throat and shouted,

"Give me an F!"

"F," the crowd shouted.

"Give me an I!" he yelled.

"I," the crowd yelled back.

"Give me a G!" he cried.

"G," the crowd cried.

"Give me an H!" he screamed.

"H," the crowd screamed.

"Give me a T!" he screamed.

"T," the crowd screeched.

Pleased with the North Dakotan response on the very first cheer, he took a deep breath and shouted as loud as he could, "WHAT'S THAT SPELL?" and was answered by complete silence.

What does it say at the top of a North Dakotan ladder?

STOP!

Did you hear about the North Dakotan who decided not to rent the "lush apartment" because he thought it was for drunks.

A wine list in a North Dakota restaurant read:
1. Red wine.
2. White wine.
(Order by number).

The doctor told the North Dakotan that his ailing wife needed some sea air. So the North Dakotan went home and fanned her with a sardine.

One good thing about being a North Dakotan— You'll never miss an important phone call because you're in the bathtub.

The North Dakotan was asked why he wore thick red suspenders.

"To keep my shoulders down."

1st North Dakotan: Whenever I'm in the dumps, I get a new hat.

2nd North Dakotan: Oh, so that's where you get them.

A North Dakotan, in the mood for joking, strolled over to a Montanan farmer working in a field and asked, "Did you happen to see a wagonload of monkeys go by?"

"Nope," said the farmer, "did you fall off?"

Teacher: "What is an autobiography?"

North Dakotan student: "Er . . . the life story of a car?"

A North Dakotan engineering student was on an elevator with a number of other passengers. As the elevator moved up, he stared at the small fan slowly turning in the elevator ceiling. "I'm amazed that such a small fan can lift all these people," he remarked to the passengers.

First North Dakotan: "Let's get us a couple of girls and go out and do the town."

Second North Dakotan: "Well, I don't know. I got a case of diarrhea."

First North Dakotan: "Bring it along, we'll drink it."

Did you hear about the North Dakotan who majored in civil engineering because he wanted to be a Roads Scholar?

A North Dakotan took, out of the library, a book with a cover which read *How to Hug* only to discover it was volume 7 of the encyclopedia.

In North Dakota if you want to learn how to cook you go to school and sign up for "home eccchhhhh."

Did you hear about the North Dakotan who went outside to watch the eclipse but quit because the moon was in the way?

A man found his North Dakotan brother hanging by his ankles in his bedroom. When asked what he was doing, the North Dakotan said, "I'm trying to commit suicide."

"You dummy," said his brother, "you're supposed to put the rope around your neck, not your ankles!"

"I tried that," said the North Dakotan, "but I couldn't breathe."

Two words you never want a North Dakotan to say to you: "Hi, neighbor."

You know you're in North Dakota when you find there are more laws regulating margarine than marijuana.

North Dakotans are so backward that when they go to order a Big Mac at McDonalds they have to order it out of the catalog.

Did you hear about the North Dakotan who went to night school so he could learn to read in the dark?

What do they call a North Dakotan who sits in a tree?
Branch Manager.

Customer standing in front of the take-out window of a fast food restaurant in Grand Forks:

"I want two hot dogs, one with mustard, one without."

North Dakotan counterman: "Which one?"

There was one caring North Dakotan who willed his body to science. Science is contesting the will.

At a North Dakotan wedding the best man was asked to sign the marriage certificate as a witness. The North Dakotan said he didn't want to get involved.

A North Dakotan from Grand Forks was recently hospitalized after playing the video game of "Pong." After winning the game the North Dakotan made the mistake of trying to jump over the net.

Did you hear about the North Dakotan who refused to read the dictionary until it was made into a movie?

The North Dakotan helicopter pilot took out his chopper on his solo flight. He ascended to 5,000 . . . 10,000 . . . 15,000 feet with no trouble. At 20,000 the control tower lost radar contact with him. Later, the wreckage was found and two weeks later the pilot regained consciousness. The doctor asked him what happened that led to his crash. The North Dakotan pilot explained, "Well, doc, I took the helicopter up to 5,000 . . . 10,000 . . . 15,000 feet. Everything was fine. But, when I got to 20,000 feet it got cold, so I shut off the fan."

One day a Montanan and a North Dakotan went deer hunting. They became separated and the Montanan did not know where the North Dakotan was until he heard shots. He headed in the direction of the shots and eventually came upon his North Dakotan hunting partner holding a rifle on another hunter. The other hunter was holding his hands over his head and pleading with the North Dakotan, "OK, you can have the deer, but can I take the saddle off first?"

WANTED: 320 acres in North Dakota to lease between November and March. Want to raise frozen vegetables.

A North Dakotan who had become aware of first aid measures came across a friend who had been injured and was bleeding from a cut lip. To stop the bleeding the North Dakotan applied a tourniquet to his friend's neck.

Milk is still delivered by a horse-drawn wagon in North Dakota. As the milkman drove by a North Dakotan's house the other day the North Dakotan yelled at the milkman, "Hey mister, you won't get home tonight. Your horse just ran out of gas."

What do you get when you cross a midget with a North Dakotan?

A short garbage man.

An affluent North Dakotan family is one that can buy twice as much cockroach powder as the family next door.

Did you hear about the North Dakotan bride who cancelled the wedding when she heard her friends were planning to give her a shower?

North Dakotans probably won't allow the sale of gasohol in their state. They're afraid it will make their headlights bloodshot.

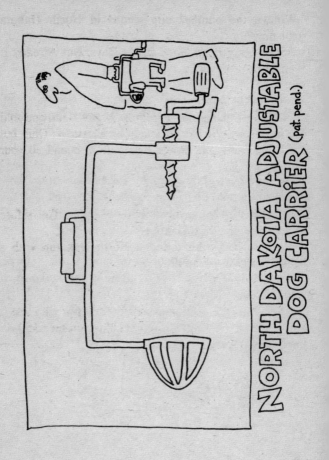

NORTH DAKOTA ADJUSTABLE DOG CARRIER (pat. pend.)

What's the number one record in North Dakota right now?

"She's Only Been Gone Seven Days, But Already It Seems Like a Week."

A North Dakotan went into the Minot Bank and told the manager, "I'd like to join your Christmas Club but I'd better warn you, I won't be able to attend all your meetings."

Why did the renowned archer William Tell refuse to do his act in North Dakota?

Because he couldn't find a North Dakotan with a head as large as his apple.

There was a North Dakotan football fan who lost a $50 bet on a TV football play. He lost another $50 on the instant replay.

What are the worst five years in the life of a North Dakotan? Third grade.

Why are there so few skyjacking attempts by North Dakotans?
What good is a parachute if you can't count to 10?

There was the North Dakotan who noticed the sign, "Wet Pavement," so he did.

You know you're in North Dakota when you see vacationers wearing thermal bikinis.

Why did the North Dakotan scratch his nose with a spoon?
He was still recuperating from his injuries when he used a fork.

North Dakotan doctor to patient who complained of a constant ringing in his ears: "Why don't you answer it?"

What is a North Dakotan symphony orchestra?
Three kazoos and a radio.

A North Dakotan opened a new business. A grand opening prize of a trip for two to the Bahamas was offered to the person who most closely could guess the number of beans in the jar. The winning North Dakotan missed the correct number of beans by only one. He guessed three beans. There were two.

A North Dakotan safari—a cockroach and a can of Raid.

Why are a North Dakotan's ears like a steam shovel? They pick up a lot of dirt.

The cloddish, but super-handsome North Dakotan movie star was finally getting his chance to make a Hollywood movie. Since he was a VIP, the most gorgeous stewardess available was assigned to look after all his needs. Batting her beautiful eyelashes, after the North Dakotan star took his seat, she said in a breathy voice: "Do you want coffee, tea—or ME?"

"Don't you have any cold sausage?" the North Dakotan asked.

A North Dakotan fifth grader in Minot was seen flipping a coin to get the answers to a true-false test. Half an hour after the other students were done, the North Dakotan boy was still flipping the coin. The teacher asked him what was taking him so long. The North Dakotan replied, "It's like you're always telling us. I'm checking my work."

There is a North Dakotan who always changes clothes in the closet because he doesn't want to undress in front of his princess phone.

A North Dakotan and a Montanan are flying from New York to Billings. The plane makes scheduled stops in Chicago, Minneapolis, Fargo and Billings. At each stop a little red truck comes out and fills the plane with fuel. As the truck pulled away from the plane in Fargo, the North Dakotan said to the Montanan, "Can you imagine how fast that guy must be driving in order to get that little red truck to every airport ahead of us?"

In North Dakota fleas are white. At least that's what the North Dakotan Mother Goose says: "Mary had a little lamb whose fleas were white as snow."

Did you hear about the North Dakotan who didn't know the difference between arson and incest? He was arrested last week for setting his sister on fire.

Two North Dakotans went to the funeral home to pay their last respects to their recently departed friend.

"He looks pretty good doesn't he?" observed one.

"He should," said the other North Dakotan. "He just got out of the hospital."

You know you're in North Dakota when you find that power brownouts in March are caused by increases in shock treatments.

Two North Dakotans went out looking for Christmas trees. They looked all day without any luck. Near nightfall one North Dakotan finally said, "The next tree we find, I'm taking, whether it has lights on it or not."

A North Dakotan heard that goats were very good for mowing the lawn. So he tried a couple of them but soon got rid of them. He found he couldn't teach them how to start the mower.

Two North Dakotans were flying a light plane one day when they saw an approaching storm.

"Hey, we better do a 360-degree turn and get out of here," said one.

Did you hear about the North Dakotan who thought a mushroom was a place to neck?

A North Dakotan was asked what he would do if his little sister swallowed the house key.

"I'd crawl in through the bedroom window."

Two Montanans and a North Dakotan were arrested for rustling cattle. The judge ordered them to be shot. As the first Montanan was being tied and blindfolded he hollered, "Tornado!" All the guards ran and hid and the Montanan escaped.

Likewise, as the second Montanan was being prepared for execution he screamed, "Watch out, flash flood!" All the guards again ran and hid and the second Montanan escaped too.

Next it was the North Dakotan's turn. From watching the Montanans' success in escaping by crying out a warning, he decided to do the same. The North Dakotan screamed, "Fire!"

Most common educational degree in North Dakota? Kindergarten dropout.

North Dakotan Pinocchio: "I had a good relationship with my nose . . . until I blew it."

North Dakotan boy: "Dad, where are the Swiss Alps?"
North Dakotan dad: "Ask your mother. She puts everything away."

You know you're in North Dakota when you realize all numbers are preceded by "ah."

Two North Dakotans went duck hunting in Montana. The Montana farmer said they could use his land and his hunting dogs. The North Dakotans hunted all day with no luck. "Sure was nice of that Montanan to let us use his land and his dogs," said one North Dakotan. "I wonder why we didn't get any ducks, though."
The other North Dakotan thought for a moment. "Do you think maybe we weren't throwing the dogs high enough?"

A sad event happened in North Dakota last week. Two North Dakotan hitchhikers were riding in the back of a pickup that went off the road and into the Souris River. The North Dakotans drowned when they weren't able to get the tailgate down.

You know you're in North Dakota when you see that the main attraction at the science museum is an 85-foot monster called "mosquitosaurus terribilitis."

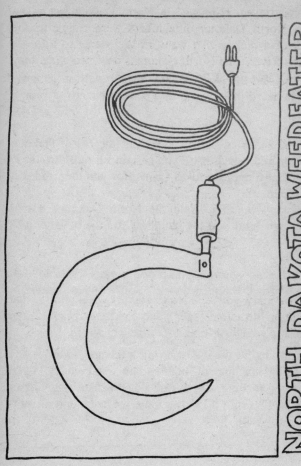

NORTH DAKOTA WEED EATER

To a North Dakotan, a camel is a horse with bucket seats.

Why did the North Dakotan water half of his lawn? He heard there was a fifty percent chance of rain.

The suffering patient looked at the North Dakotan doctor and asked, "Are you certain I'll pull through? I heard of a man who was treated for jaundice and died of diphtheria."

"Don't be silly," said the North Dakotan doctor. "When I treat you for jaundice, you die of jaundice!"

A freezer salesman was trying to close a sale and told the North Dakotan woman, "You'll save a fortune on your food bills."

"I won't argue with you," said the North Dakotan, "but we're already saving a fortune with our new car by not taking a bus. We're saving a fortune with our new washing machine by not sending out laundry. We're saving a fortune with our new dishwasher by giving up the maid. Truth is, at this time, we just can't afford to save any more."

Did you hear about the North Dakotan who wanted to be a tree surgeon but couldn't stand the sight of sap?

Did you hear about the North Dakotan lawyer who wouldn't hang wallpaper in his house until it had a fair trial?

There was a North Dakotan who couldn't decide what to wear to the masquerade party. Finally, after much thought, he stole one of Dolly Parton's old sweaters and went as a camel.

The whole scientific community was electrified the other day when the world famous North Dakotan Research Institute announced its latest technical advance: a steam powered computer.

Did you hear about the North Dakotan who applied for a job as a lifeguard in a car wash?

North Dakotan Health Warning:
If you feel pressure on your head, your eyes are almost pressed shut and you smell an unusual odor and one foot is cold . . . you have your sock over your head.

A North Dakotan appeared at the police station one day and said he wanted to register a complaint.

"I've got three brothers," he explained. "We all live in one small apartment. One of my brothers has six rats. Another has eight dogs, and the third has a goat. The smell in there is just awful. I'd like to do something about it."

"Doesn't your apartment have any windows?" the policeman asked.

"Well, of course it has," the North Dakotan answered.

"Then open them," the policeman suggested.

The North Dakotan looked embarrassed and a little confused. "And lose all my pigeons?" he said.

You know you're in North Dakota when you see a hitchhiker with a sign that reads, "Anywhere but here."

A formal North Dakotan dinner is where all the men wear clean tee-shirts.

It simply isn't true that North Dakotans use bath water to make North Dakotan beer. In fact, there isn't enough bath water in all of North Dakota to make a single case of suds. For North Dakotan beer they use dishwater.

For those not familiar with North Dakotan eating habits, the "higher priced spread" referred to in the North Dakotan TV commercial is known to the rest of of us as lard.

A North Dakotan married his ex-wife's sister so that he wouldn't have to break in a new mother-in-law.

A satisfied diner was speaking to the chef of a fine restaurant in Bismarck: "Your sauce is divine, but tell me, how much wine does it use?"
North Dakotan chef: "About a mouthful."

Mental patient to North Dakotan psychiatrist: "All the time I keep stuffing my nose with pipe tobacco."
North Dakotan psychiatrist: "Want a light?"

A North Dakotan's Dilemma....